THE
POWER
OF
ONE

Authentic Leadership in Turbulent Times

Sharif M. Abdullah

NEW SOCIETY PUBLISHERS

Library of Congress Cataloging-in-Publication Data:
Abdullah, Sharif M.
    The power of one : authentic leadership in turbulent times / Sharif
M. Abdullah.
        p.   cm.
    ISBN 0-86571-324-3. — ISBN 0-86571-325-1 (pbk.)
    1. Conduct of life. 2. Social values. 3. Leadership. 4. Power
(Philosophy) 5. United States—Moral conditions—Miscellanea. I.
Title.
BF1595.A23 1995   158'.4—dc20   95-16194

Inquiries regarding requests to reprint all or part of *The Power of One:
Authentic Leadership in Turbulent Times* should be addressed to New
Society Publishers, P.O. Box 189, Gabriola Island, BC V0R 1X0.
    ISBN Hardcover   USA 0-86571-324-3   CAN 1-55092-272-6
    ISBN Paperback   USA 0-86571-325-1   CAN 1-55092-273-4

Cover design by Margie Politzer. Book design by Martin Kelley. Printed
on partially-recycled paper using soy-based ink by Capital City Press of
Montpelier, Vermont.

To order directly from the publisher, add $3.00 to the price for the first
copy, and add $1.00 (plus GST in Canada) for each additional copy. Send
check or money order to:
    New Society Publishers
    PO Box 189, Gabriola Island, BC Canada V0R 1X0

New Society Publishers aims to publish books for fundamental social
change through nonviolent action. We focus especially on sustainable
living, progressive leadership, and educational and parenting resources.
Our on-line catalog is available for browsing at: www.newsociety.com

NEW SOCIETY PUBLISHERS
Gabriola Island, BC and Stony Creek, CT

Table of Contents

When our days become dreary with low-hovering clouds and our nights become darker than a thousand midnights, we will know that we are living in the creative turmoil of a genuine civilization struggling to be born.
                              —Martin Luther King, Jr.

Introduction

Reading this book is a subversive act. Not subversive in the sense that I'll teach you how to become a terrorist, or give you the plans for home-made pipe bombs. It is subversive like the Civil Rights campaigns of Martin Luther King, Jr., the fight for India's independence of Mahatma Gandhi, the Greenbelt Movement of Kenya's Wangari Maathai, the Velvet Revolution of Czechoslovakia's Vaclav Havel.

We spend our time in frustration, protest and anger, because we have not encompassed the power of one committed person. We have created a system out of control, too large and complex for any of us to comprehend. Every day, by our every action, we support, prop up, bolster that system. Even those who take to the streets in protest against the injustices of that system give it unwitting support through their acknowledgment of its power.

An individual, acting alone, acting from the depths of their commitment, can change the world. That is something "the system" does not want you to think about. It is a subversive thought.

It took a long time for me to conduct the lectures which comprise the body of this book. I felt unqualified to talk about leadership and power. I wanted someone else to come forward and write this. I didn't feel that I had worked out my personal "stuff." I have fears; I have doubts; I have weaknesses.

I felt I had to get my challenges worked out before I was qualified to speak.

However, the conditions we face on this small planet are not waiting for us to get our acts together. We are forced to "get it together" within the context of the crisis. So I had to come to grips with the fact that I may not be ready, I may still have challenges, but it is time to act nonetheless.

Almost everyone reading this is in the same boat. You are unsure, uncertain, trying to make sense of turbulent times. You may feel unprepared, but ready or not, here comes the Third Millennium.

The time has come for a new understanding of power and leadership. The old ways simply don't work anymore. The old explanations don't explain anything. As someone recently said, the world events we face are too important to leave to the politicians.

Our current system is no longer adequate for our needs. Our society has gotten far too complex for any one person to understand. We act, having no idea *why* we act.

We fumble around, looking for direction, as we head closer to the chasm. In a time of chaos, we see all of the dangers and none of the opportunities.

We drift, bickering, fighting, arguing about who is to blame for the present morass. All of us must share the blame. We spend much time focusing on the immensity of the problem, trying to assign blame; we are reluctant to focus on a solution.

We fail because deep down inside we don't feel the problem even has a solution. We propose alternatives as a gesture, out of guilt, with the deep belief that nothing will change for our efforts.

We continue to place implicit faith and trust in institutions which constantly fail us. We do this, because the alternative is to admit our own failures.

This simply must stop.

The times call for a revolution. A revolution in consciousness. That is the purpose of this book.

Notes to the Reader:

Gender

In an attempt to balance our unfortunately sexist language with readability, I have alternated masculine and feminine pronouns in paragraphs throughout the text. (Those of you compulsive enough to count the number of times I use each pronoun should know I do not share your compulsion; the count "feels" right.)

"America"

In several places in this book I refer to "America" and "Americans." I want to clarify these references.

What I mean by "American" is *not* a reference to people who live in the United States or people who are defined as US citizens. (In the text, I refer to US citizens as such.) If my definition was geographic, "American" would include Canadians, Mexicans and others in North, Central and South America.

What I mean by "American" is a *culture*, including a mind-set. Not all people who are US citizens share this culture and mind-set; in fact, "Americans" are probably in the minority. When the culture of "Americans" gets confused as representing a political structure, we lose sight of it as a culture.

We know the culture of "Americans." It is Western European-based, culturally chauvinistic and isolationist as most cultures are. We could explore the "American" mind-set regarding typical cultural elements like language, gender relationships, authority patterns, etc. However, like any other culture, you know it when you see it. Like every other culture, when you are within it, you call it "normal."

And this culture is valid, as all cultures are. Our job is to celebrate the appropriate parts and help transform the inappropriate. Of course, that means being willing to do the same with whatever our culture is.

Part One

Mega-Crisis and Global Chaos

What Is a Crisis?

What is a crisis? Do I have a crisis when I can't find a parking space? When the phone rings at 5:00 in the morning and I don't want to get up?

Dangerous Opportunity

Asian languages are constructed in a way that gives an enhanced meaning to everyday words. In Chinese, the pictogram for the word *crisis* is "dangerous opportunity." The two words are joined, "danger" and "opportunity."

In sometimes mysterious ways, a crisis creates the tension point from which we act. The purpose of a crisis is to point us in a direction, to show us the danger and to point us to an opportunity. There are actions we would not take unless faced with a problem. We look at a dwindling bank account and suddenly we are doing something about it. What we call "mid-life crisis" is a call to expand to a larger sense of self.

Years ago, I had an opportunity to speak with the CEO of Burger King. He said that the impetus to start Burger King came when he was fired from a mid-level executive position at McDonald's. He thought he was going to have a career with McDonald's for the rest of his life; all of a sudden, he was facing a crisis. He found himself middle-aged, out of work, with his only marketable skill selling hamburgers. So he decided to go into business for himself selling hamburgers. The rest is history.

A crisis creates the tension point from which we act.

He was able to use a situation which for him was dangerous. He was compelled to do something about it. He was able to seize the opportunity inherent in the crisis.

Frog Soup

Everybody knows the recipe for Frog Soup: one frog, boiling water, season to taste. But, if you drop a live frog into boiling water, it jumps right out. You have to put the live frog in lukewarm water; it will just sit there comfortably. Then you slowly raise it to a boil. By the time the water starts to boil, the frog will be so damaged it won't be able jump out.

I use this rather gruesome example to illustrate a point. We are all frogs. We are now the prime ingredient in global Frog Soup. Things are getting worse and worse. The quality of our lives is slowly deteriorating. And, if we don't "jump" soon, we will reach the point of no return. This, our lives and challenges of the 1990s, is our "dangerous opportunity."

What Is a Mega-Crisis?

Many of the problems we face are truly global in nature. These problems are creating the conditions which cry out for change. Our question is: what do we do about it? In which direction do we "jump?"

Think back to the last presidential election. Do you remember the issues that were discussed during that election? The candidates debated the burning issues of our time; things like whether or not you were saluting the American flag, who was tougher on crime, who was going to give the biggest tax break to the rich. Totally meaningless non-issues. They never discussed the issues that are coming to a boil, turning us all into Frog Soup.

The crises which we face are so large, so complex, so interconnected I call them "mega-crises." These issues exist to jolt us out of our sense of complacency and propel us to opportunities we can scarcely see.

A mega-crisis has certain definable properties:

1. Whether directly or indirectly, a mega-crisis affects everyone on the planet.

2. A mega-crisis happens slowly, over decades. It is not something that Dan Rather can spew in a 30 second news bite on the six o'clock news. And, because it is so big, the mega-crisis remains relatively invisible to the mainstream

media. What gets reported in the media are the symptoms of the mega-crisis, not the mega-crisis itself.

3. A mega-crisis is impervious to all current means of analysis and resolution. A mega-crisis cannot be resolved through current methods of dispute resolution. A mega-crisis cannot be understood by linear analysis. A mega-crisis cannot be resolved through the use of force.

4. Each mega-crisis is interconnected with every other mega-crisis. The mega-crises form a fabric; pulling on one thread moves the whole fabric. Attempts to isolate and resolve a mega-crisis only make things worse.

> ## *A mega-crisis cannot be resolved through current methods of dispute resolution.*

5. A mega-crisis shatters society and threatens our well-being. It makes us stand up and pay attention. Take for example the CEO of Burger King; if instead of being fired, he was just demoted, or denied an annual raise, he'd still be sitting at McDonald's. The mega-crisis makes us think that our world is coming apart. Ignore it, and the world will indeed come apart.

6. Because it is potent, the mega-crisis is our primary cause of denial. Because of the nature of the society we have created, we all are in some level of denial. A mega-crisis makes us look at ourselves, and we don't like what we see. When the picture is really ugly, we lock into denial; it doesn't really exist.

7. A mega-crisis creates the energy for a paradigm shift. The mega-crisis aids in the search for a paradigm shift, from one pattern of being to another.

Global Chaos

The Nature of Chaos

If a crisis represents a specific event, a certain dangerous opportunity, chaos is the non-specific accumulation of crises. In a crisis, once you fix it, once you weather the storm, it is over and you can go back to living your life, changed in some perhaps profound way, but you again reach "normal."

Chaos is not like that. "Normal" has gone away forever. Things will never be the same again. Take for example the peasants in France and America in the 1770s: "normal" is working hard, paying taxes to the crown, living a simple life. Along come the democratic revolutions which bring sweeping changes, competing loyalties, expanded responsibilities, new allegiances, a frightening array of options and opportunities. The end of "normal."

Chaos is the non-specific accumulation of crises.

Or consider the black slave in the 1860s: "normal" was a brutal world of work, orders and beatings. Existing in that world was a matter of doing what you were told, keeping a low profile and praying for a master who was not totally psychotic. Then comes Emancipation. Along with the freedom that every human spirit yearns for comes a bewildering array of choices, opportunities and new dangers. After over one hundred years, some of the descendants of those slaves have not yet emerged from that chaos to create a sense of positive identity.

The times we face today are equally daunting. The period of chaos we have already entered will dwarf all those faced by our ancestors. We are being called upon to re-make our consciousness, to do so in the face of a tidal wave of problems so great we have difficulty comprehending them.

There is no way out of the global chaos. *There is no way out of the global chaos.* I repeat the sentence, since many of you went into denial upon reading it. Here is an analogy: your basement is flooded; water is starting to move into your living room and kitchen. You receive reliable reports that your entire house will be under water and will stay that way forever. You have about a day to decide what to do.

Mr. and Mrs. Denial will sit tight. They may move some of their furniture to the second floor, but basically they will deny that the problem merits drastic action. When pressed, they will say that even if they believed that chaos was about to engulf them, they would act no differently; they would rather not face living in a changed world.

There is no way out of global chaos.

The Doubter family is actively building a dike of sandbags around their house, pumping out the basement, and loading supplies for the long haul. They believe that the chaos is real, but instead of changing themselves, they have decided to fight the chaos. (During the last oil embargo, Mr. Doubter built a 10,000 gallon storage facility in his backyard instead of carpooling.) "By God, we're going to get through this thing with our lifestyles intact, if I have to build a wall 100 feet tall

all around my house!" The Doubter family does not have enough sandbags for a 200 foot wall.

The Noah Family is preparing for adventure. Mr. Noah is preparing a boat with long-term rations; Ms. Noah is deciding what are the most essential items to take with them to their new lifestyle. They are looking back with nostalgia and forward with anticipation. They are ready to float on top of chaos.

The Five Mega-Crises

There are many prophecies about the world ending in a rain of fire and brimstone, or floods, or other disasters. The events in our current "end of the world" drama occur so slowly that it takes a special perception to even see that there is a problem. What follows represents my window on the unfolding drama.

These are presented in no particular order; each is equally important. However, I do put the ecological crisis in the middle. I do this to emphasize that the ecological crisis is no more (or less) important than the others.

The web we weave is increasingly toxic, hostile to the human spirit. Our actions form the walls of our prison.

The environment is "in." We all talk about the ecological crisis, saving the planet, etc. The current fads have schoolchildren recycling, homemakers taking expensive designer bags to the grocery store instead of using paper bags, etc. The ecological mega-crisis is crucially important, but it can also be a bit of a smokescreen. Some people latch on to the ecological crisis so that they can avoid the others. There are plenty of folks out there saving the whales, but not addressing any of the other four crises. Their actions are futile; they will not be able to solve the ecological crisis without recognizing and acting on the others.

> **It is virtually impossible to discuss mega-crises in a linear fashion.**

Given the interconnected nature of the mega-crises, it is virtually impossible to discuss them in a linear fashion. The charts which follow attempt a more global, holistic representation of the mega-crises than a narrative would suggest. My purpose is to give some indication of the seamless web of interactions.

As depicted in Figure One, our mega-crises rest upon the bed of our consciousness. Our consciousness creates our culture, it creates the way that we see the world. Our world view, our values and beliefs combine to create our institutions, our political, economic and social systems.

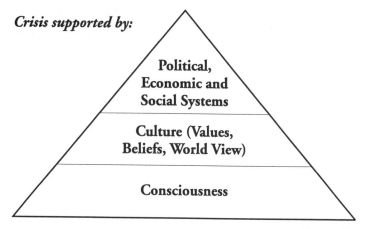

Crisis supported by:

Political, Economic and Social Systems

Culture (Values, Beliefs, World View)

Consciousness

Figure One

People who blame former president George Bush for the Persian Gulf War are mistaken. The Persian Gulf War came from the dysfunctional consciousness most people in the United States hold. President Bush was not a cause, but a reflection. The majority of people in the United States believe the use of force to resolve conflict is okay, just as the majority of citizens at one time thought it was proper to enslave other human beings. Group thought is not necessarily good thought.

In the past, we have attempted to change political and economic systems without first changing the underlying consciousness.

In the past, we have attempted to change political and economic systems without first changing the underlying consciousness supporting these systems. Once we shift the underlying consciousness, issues of culture start to become more visible. Once we transform consciousness and culture, the political, economic and social systems will change overnight.

This was the work of King and Gandhi, changing the consciousness which undergirds the seemingly invincible institutions of colonialism and apartheid.

The dominant consciousness paradigm of our society is "I Am Separate." Even people who are committed to ecology and peace movements continue to hold to the "I Am Separate" consciousness pattern. Seeing oneself separate from other individuals and separate from the environment creates the culture of racism, sexism and other modes of oppression and class consciousness.

The emerging consciousness is "We Are One." I s
as interrelated and interdependent with all others a.....
the environment. I see each of us as a reflection of the other.
The emerging paradigm creates the concept of community.
The emerging paradigm supports the institutions of
democracy and social justice.

When a society attempts to change its institutions without
first changing the underlying consciousness, we wind up with
affirmative action regulations, formalistic quotas and set-
asides, environmental bean-counting, all to be swept aside
and forgotten at the first opportunity. Changing
consciousness will cause the real, meaningful and lasting
institutional changes to occur.

Mega-Crisis Chart

Chart One defines our mega-crises the things that are
sending our world into global chaos.

We are in the middle of the global chaos, right now. It is
not something that is "going to happen." It is now happening.
Our society is falling like a centuries old Douglas Fir tree; the
fall appears to be happening slowly, but that is because it has
a long way to fall.

In Chart One, issues like homelessness, drugs, abortion,
and patriotism are listed as symptoms, not root issues.
Stopping the drug trade will not end drug use, because the
drug trade is merely a symptom of the mega-crisis of personal
fulfillment. Similarly, stopping water and air pollution will
not in itself stop the destruction of Planet Earth, since it is
only a part of the overall mega-crisis of the ecology.

In Figure Two, we see the mega-crises interconnected into
a model of global chaos. Each mega-crisis is connected to each
other; it is impossible to affect one without affecting the

Chart One—The Mega-Crises

Economy

The "Haves" vs. "Have-nots": the growing disparity between the super-rich and the super-poor.

1. Malappropriated resources;
2. instability/collapse of global markets;
3. gross disparities between super-rich and ultra-poor;
4. tax structures which benefit the wealthy;
5. basic human needs unmet;
6. growth-model economic system based on continued exploitation of rapidly depleted resources.

Diversity

"Them" vs. "Us": ethnicity, cultural diversity and national identity in conflict.

1. Growing ethnic and racial clashes;
2. the rapid growth of "hate groups";
3. the surfacing of long-buried cultural prejudices and animosities;
4. extinction of cultures.

Ecology

The Destruction of Planet Earth: the danger of ecological systems failure.

1. Pollution (introduction of waste into the Earth's eco-system beyond its carrying capacity);
2. overconsumption (resource depletion beyond the Earth's ability to regenerate);
3. mechanistic approaches to the management of living systems.

Fulfillment

The Addictive Society: the search for personal, social and spiritual fulfillment.

1. Crimes of violence (attempt to inject personal power into a situation of apparent powerlessness);
2. dwindling hope;
3. drugs and other forms of addictive behavior;
4. spiritual, personal and societal malaise;
5. shallow patriotism;
6. rise in birth rate among poor.

Leadership

The Crisis of Global Leadership: dangerous opportunity and whistling in the dark.

1. Use of "leadership" in a vain attempt to maintain status quo;
2. attempts to maintain "power-over";
3. empty symbolism and non-issues;
4. lack of vision;
5. militarism in all its forms; the use of force to resolve conflicts;
6. political alienation, people removed from their "leaders";
7. dependence on complacency, acquiescence and focusing on non-issues.

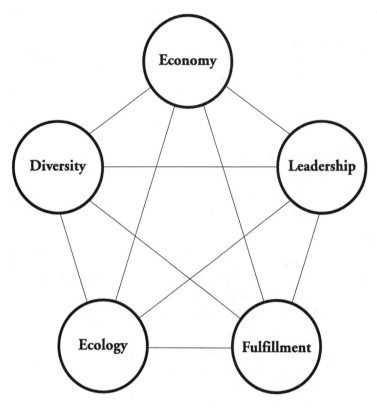

Figure Two

others. A change in consciousness in Leadership will positively affect Ecology, which will affect the Economy, which will affect Fulfillment....

In Figures Three and Four, we see how the global chaos model can be used to analyze domestic and international problems. Linear analysis has been used to explain and justify actions which, using the global chaos model, are plainly inadequate, irrelevant and perhaps even counter-productive.

These words are attributed to Chief Seattle:

Figure Three—War and Peace

Humankind has not woven the web of life. We are but one thread within it. Whatever we do to the web, we do to ourselves. All things are bound together. All things connect. Whatever befalls the Earth befalls also the children of the Earth.

As depicted in the charts, the web we weave is increasingly toxic, increasingly hostile to the human spirit. Our actions form the walls of our prison.

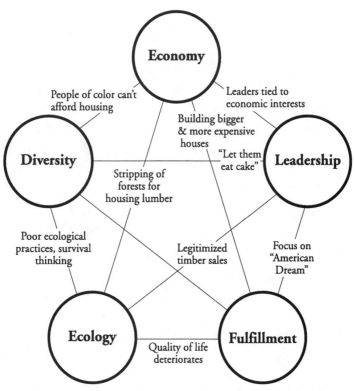

Figure Four—Homelessness

Part Two

Slow Motion Armageddon

The Inadequacy of Current Notions of Power and Leadership

The Old Power Responses

Our current leadership is plagued by linear, hierarchical, left-brain thinking. Linear thinking can only see and respond to immediate, short-term, "cause and effect" problems. The mega-crises which make up global chaos happen so slowly they are difficult to see.

When faced with a crisis, our current leadership exhibits habitual responses which get in the way of effective action. These habitual responses include:

Withdrawal/Denial

What problem? There is no problem. Our forests die, our lakes and streams become poisoned, the marble is eaten off of the faces of our buildings by acid rain—and government leaders call for still more study, denying there is a problem. They will never acknowledge the problem, even when acid rain eats away the White House.

Or, for example, the Japanese whaling industry continues the slaughter of the whales; it will cease "studying" the problem when there are no more whales left to study.

Operating from Limited Self-Interest or Factionalism

If there is a biological or chemical war going on, the old leadership isn't interested in stopping it—they just want to sell the gas masks. Some of us are not invested in stopping war, just in making a profit from the masks.

If that sounds facetious, think about the argument that some Oregon recyclers used in shooting down a citizen initiative against wasteful over-packaging: "if you ban waste, I won't have enough material to recycle."

Another example: the Department of Housing and Urban Development exists in part to build housing for people who do not have adequate housing. But when seen through the lens of self-interest, HUD is primarily a subsidy program for developers.

Blaming/Making Wrong/ Separating/Creating the Enemy

If there is a problem, assign blame. That of course does absolutely nothing to solve the problem, but at least you can absolve yourself by pointing the finger at the Democrats/ Republicans / liberals / conservatives / environmentalists/ industrialists… somebody other than me.

> **Every year the members of Congress point their fingers at each other in blame. And every year they are right.**

Look at the continuing budget "crisis" in Congress. Passing a congressional budget rises to the level of Kabuki theater. Every year they go through the same dance, the same wailing, the same hand-wringing. Every year the members of Congress on both sides of the aisle point their fingers at each other in blame. And every year, both sides are right.

In its extreme blaming is creating an enemy. For decades, people in the United States defined themselves by what they were against: communism. We could label everything we were afraid of, everything we did not understand, everything that kept us from having our way with the world as "communist."

With the internal collapse of the communist economic and political systems, we faced the need to either come to grips with our own shortcomings, or create a new enemy. All of a sudden, Saddam Hussein became America's "enemy." Those same "leaders" who claimed he was worse than Hitler and waged all out war were supporting him a few months earlier! Americans would rather fabricate an enemy than face an identity crisis.

Controlling Behavior

Is there an environmental problem? I will control the behavior. I will control the spawning of fish in the Columbia River. I will manipulate the genes of trees, so that they will grow when, where and how I dictate. And, in the face of nature's contrary intentions, I will exercise still more control.

Years ago, a tropical island experienced a mosquito infestation. Instead of looking for a natural balance, the western aid workers bombarded the area with DDT, a highly poisonous substance. It killed the mosquitoes. It also poisoned the birds and lizards, and subsequently it killed all the cats on the island, which ate the birds and lizards. The island then experienced a rat population out of control; the aid workers had to parachute cats into the area to keep the rats from overrunning the villages on the island. This was a classic case of the "cure" being worse than the disease.

The ultimate in control is the police action. The ultimate authority of government rests in the power to kill another. The threat of killing another provides a level of control over their behavior: "you will act thusly or else...."

The police response to a mega-crisis is an empty gesture. Police actions are used to punish instead of correct. Neither the police nor the politicians really expect behavior to change; they are venting their own feelings and frustrations; they are expressing the societal disease. Look at the inner city police behavior toward drug use. In North and South America, police will "reward" the "good" drug addicts with money and drugs for information and subservience, while "punishing" the "bad" drug addicts who resist their authority. In some US urban centers, the police department is the largest single dispenser of controlled, dangerous drugs.

The Inadequacy of Old Notions of Power

The old notions of power are ineffectual; old power never addresses the mega-crises; old power evades crises. The outmoded concepts of power are totally inadequate to respond to the world we face today.

Someone once said that if you only have a hammer you tend to see all of your problems as nails. If all we have is knee-jerk, controlling responses, we will continue to look to linear, patriarchal, militaristic solutions to holistic challenges.

Part Three

Authentic Power as a Spiritual Practice

Cats and Rats

A few years ago, I experienced a recurring dream. In my waking life, I faced severe economic problems. The elements of the recurring dream were always the same; there were always a cat and a rat.

The rats were very detailed and very distinct. They were three or four feet high, they would sit up on their hind legs, they were well-muscled, and I could see every hair on their bodies. They looked very intelligent, with questing eyes. The cats were always very lethargic, most of the time they couldn't even stand up. They would lie in puddles on the floor. They were indistinct; I couldn't tell head from tail.

Night after night, I would have this dream. Super-articulated rats and indistinct, weak cats. Finally, I realized what the dreams meant. The rats were my debts, the problems in my life at that time. I focused on my debts, I looked at them, I analyzed them. I would round up my bills and go through them, add them, worry over them. I dwelled on the debts; I fixated on them.

The cats were my abundance, my resources. I paid no attention to them. They were lethargic.

As soon as I realized the meaning of the dream, I asked myself: what are my assets? What is my abundance? I sat down and made a list of my spiritual, physical and financial assets. By the time I finished with the list, I saw the solution to my pressing debt problem. My answer to my financial crisis was right in front of me all the time. I couldn't see it when I was preoccupied with focusing on the problems.

The next night, I had a dream. The dream was about a beautiful black cat: huge, sleek, powerful. And, there was a little tiny mouse scurrying along the floor.

We all do this; we all tend to focus on the problems instead of the solution. And in doing this, we ignore or deny the solution, or at least deny the possibility of solution.

Creating a solution also creates the responsibility for implementing the solution.

I sit in meetings of people who very correctly see and analyze the mega-crises. They analyze and re-analyze. They issue reports and studies. These are the same people who come up to me and (quite proudly) recite the latest military atrocity or ecological catastrophe or social travesty.

These committed individuals stare blankly when I ask them to articulate their solution. At best, their stated solution is making someone else act.

We focus on the rats while avoiding the cats because creating a solution also creates the *responsibility* for implementing the solution. We want someone else to do that. The Democrats want the Republicans to come up with the solution, so they can shoot it down. The blacks want the whites to come up with the solution, so they can criticize it.

Changing focus from problems to solutions, from rats to cats, takes willpower. And nothing else.

What Is Authentic Power?

What is the nature of authentic power? If, for example, I reach into my briefcase, draw a pistol, hold it to your head, and order you to take me to the supermarket, does that give me power over you?

In our inner cities, armies of well-armed, angry youth, black, white, Latino and Asian, are trying to exhibit power in the world by shooting at one another. Whether based on their gang insignia, the neighborhood in which they live, or the color of their skin, each incident is an attempt to inject power into a frustrating, powerless situation.

One must command oneself before commanding others. (Fortune Cookie)

In Chinese, the character for "power" has three elements. One part is forward motion; the second part is a heart; the third part is a goal. Therefore, the Chinese definition of power is moving forward, with heart, to achieve a goal. When you have all three elements, heart, forward motion, and a goal, you are beginning to achieve authentic power. If you do something without heart, without love, it lacks power. If you act without a goal, you act without power.

30

Based on this definition, we can see why in the United States angry armed youth will never achieve power. What is their goal? Where is their heart? What is the forward motion? And the same questions can be asked of our government representatives as we watch Congress drifting about in circles.

Power and Responsibility

Power and responsibility are connected. If you choose not to take responsibility, you cannot have power. The opposite is true also; if you accept responsibility, you will find yourself with power. President Harry Truman, who took over the leadership of this country under troubling circumstances, had a plaque made for his desk: "The Buck Stops Here." Most of the presidents of the past few decades have tried to blame their own failures on the other party. They ought to have plaques made for their desks that read "The Buck Stops Somewhere Over There."

In our personal lives, we are unwilling to take responsibility, and therefore, give our power to someone else. Sometimes, it doesn't even matter to whom we relinquish our power.

When I was in Czechoslovakia directly after the "Velvet Revolution," conferring with people at Civic Forum, I was surprised to find that, in their first free election in forty years, the people of Czechoslovakia almost returned the Communist Party to power. Why? Many citizens voted for the Communists because they would "take care of you." They would not hold you responsible for anything; they would take care of everything. Everyone agreed that the Communists were terrible at governing, but at least they were willing to govern. Civic Forum, on the other hand, promised that each Czechoslovakian would be personally responsible for what happened in the future. Civic Forum would only create the space for the solutions to emerge from within.

Things will continue to get worse until enough of us wake up and take charge.

When we look at various communities within the United States, we see that many people lack the sense of power as personal responsibility. People grumble and groan but basically go along with the program. I look at the number of times blacks, who could support a strong, progressive candidate for elective office, instead opt for one who will continue the status quo. Many people seem to think it is better to have a bad solution which is someone else's responsibility than to risk personal responsibility.

The mega-crises that consume us—the environment, ethnic strife, fiscal madness—exist for one reason: to get us out of seeing ourselves as powerless and irresponsible. Things will continue to get worse until enough of us wake up and take charge. Things will continue to get worse until *you* assume the responsibility of leadership.

All of us who created the problem must take responsibility for solving it.

All of us who created the problem (through either our action or our inaction) must take responsibility for solving it. We must be the pioneers of a new social order. Not by narrowly focusing on special interests like animal rights or ethnic issues or abortion: these are just sub-sets of the larger mega-crises. We must adopt a new paradigm which speaks to the dawning of a new day for us all.

We must commit ourselves to living the vision of a fulfilling society now. We must show others that there indeed is hope for a future which works for us all. We must work for a world without enemies. Everything we do, our every act, can be a positive step toward that vision. It is the least we can do for our planet. It is the least we can do for ourselves.

Part Four
The Power of the Spirit

The Power of People

Mobilizing the Power of People

We have power to change our lives. We have power to nurture and support our children. We have power to help our neighbors, our community and our planet.

We each can be models of authentic leadership, right now, in our personal and private lives. We each can demonstrate the principles of authentic, heart-centered leadership, as we exercise leadership with our children, our classmates, our co-workers, our neighbors.

The most potent force on the planet today is the power of mobilized people. It is also the one most unused.

Years ago, I was touring an impacted area of Charlotte, North Carolina with Ron Leeper, a city councilman. We were stopped by a resident who asked Mr. Leeper what the city was going to do about the trash in the street. He asked her, "Who put the trash there?" Startled by his question, the woman answered, "My next door neighbor." Ron replied, "Did you ask her to stop?"

His question, while not denying the responsibility of the city to clean the streets, helped the woman see that she was not powerless to change the situation.

I ask that same question when I do empowerment work in impacted areas. When people complain about drug dealers, my question is, "Did you ask them to stop? Have you looked them in the eye, made human to human contact with them, and asked them to change their behavior? Without anger, without judgment, without putting them down, without making a logical argument—just ask them to stop."

This is the most potent force on the planet today: the power of mobilized people. It is also the one most unused.

Look at the number of times mobilized, motivated, committed people have utterly defeated the overwhelming military might arrayed against them. From the "People Power" revolution in the Philippines, which toppled the Marcos regime, to the overthrow of the Shah of Iran, to the dismantling of the Berlin Wall, people around the world have used courage and determination to reshape their lives.

The other side of the "people power" coin is powerless militancy. When I practiced law, an acquaintance of mine came to me for consultation. "I want you to sue the school system for failing to educate my son." She went on to explain that her fifteen year old son was reading well below his grade level, and that he was constantly under suspension or other school punishment. I took notes furiously as she cited statistics of the number of black youth under suspension, the racial disparity of grade point averages and reading levels, etc.

The other side of the "people power" coin is powerless militancy.

When I could, I squeezed in a question. "What was the cause of his last suspension?"

"I told you, they're a bunch of racists. They'll do anything to keep a young black man back."

My pencil hesitated. "That may be true, but they would not say the reason for his suspension was because he was black. What reason did they give for the suspension."

She crossed her arms in front of her. "Well, *they* said they found drugs in his locker."

"Did they in fact find any drugs?" I felt like I was cross-examining my own client.

"Well, yes. You know, that was probably an illegal search and seizure of his locker, wasn't it?"

During the course of the rest of that fairly painful interview, I learned that her son had been found with drugs and weapons several times on school property, was indeed far behind his fellow students, but was recognized as bright by his teachers, who kept giving him "one more chance."

His mother was in complete denial regarding her role and responsibility. The instability of her intimate relationships, her own casual drug use, her inattentiveness as a custodial parent—according to her, none of these things had an impact on her son's life choices. Once she sued the school system, everything would be fine. Her militancy masked her lack of responsibility.

I declined to initiate the lawsuit. I strongly urged her to seek counseling, including drug counseling, for both herself and her son. She never spoke to me again.

The opposite of my former client's behavior is that of John Woolman, a Quaker who lived during the 1700s in colonial America. In reading about that period, I was shocked to find that Quakers in the early days of this country owned slaves. Woolman thought that the ownership of another human being was a violation of religious and human decency. He was one of the first Quakers to act on this realization. He went to many of the slave-holding Quakers, over the course of several decades, quietly talking, convincing, persuading.

Just one man in a wagon, visiting distant farms throughout the thirteen colonies, meeting with people one at a time, going back to those who were not convinced several times. He continued this work throughout his life and eventually, Quakers did not own slaves as a matter of principle. Woolman's quiet actions helped to change the culture of the Quakers. His actions anticipated Quaker assistance in the Underground Railroad, the Civil Rights movement, and continuing on to this day in the American Friends Service Committee. Millions have benefited from his quiet, gentle determination.

> **We each are less than a footnote in history. We each possess the power to persuade, the power to call others to compassion.**

John Woolman is less than a footnote in history, but his actions helped make this planet a better place, helped make us more human.

We each are less than a footnote in history. We each possess the same power as John Woolman: the power to persuade, to model the values we profess, to use compassionate power to call others to be accountable for their actions.

The Power of Personal Choice

There was a mini-culture in the northeast Portland neighborhood I inhabited on moving to Oregon. We tended to leave our porch lights on most of the night and our window shades open to street view. It gave a really nice, warm feeling to the neighborhood. In some very subtle way, my neighbors were able to influence my behavior. Although I tend to be a very private person, since being influenced by these neighbors, I turn on the porch light and leave open my shades at night.

We are developing a culture, a consciousness of global responsibility.

No one, at any point in time, came up and said, "In this neighborhood, you leave your porch light on and your drapes open." Or, "There's a five dollar fine for not turning on your porch light." It just is the norm, the culture, what we expect from each other. We all accept it and reinforce it.

Tom Potter, former Police Chief in Portland, told me a similar story about his experience in Japan. While on an exchange visit, he was riding with a Japanese police team when they spotted a man beginning to jaywalk across the street. (In a city like Tokyo, with its millions of people, few residents jaywalk.) The police cruiser turned on its lights, and the man scurried back on the sidewalk, bowing low as the police passed. Impressed, Potter asked how big the fine was for jaywalking in Japan. The Japanese police replied, "There is no fine for jaywalking; it's not against the law. We just reminded that man of his duty."

Someone said, "Culture is what you don't pay any attention to." Culture is the given, it's what you don't see. We are developing a culture, a consciousness of global responsibility. We are moving away from a culture of wastefulness and self-absorption, to a culture where we are mindful of our duty to each other and to the planet.

Cultural change even affects corporate culture. An executive for a large Portland corporation recently told me about a "small success" within their corporate ranks. A group of ecologically conscious employees began a successful recycling campaign within the organization. One of them thought to ask the corporation's customers to recycle printed material sent to them, instead of just throwing it in the trash for the landfill. To their dismay, the employees discovered the corporation's brightly colored orange and blue envelopes were unrecyclable. The employees then decided to switch to a plain envelope made out of recycled paper, a move which saved the company thousands of dollars in printing costs and saved the environment literally tons of waste in a landfill. Said the executive, "Decades ago, somebody thought blue and orange envelopes were cute; nobody ever questioned that decision once made. We are now looking into other areas where we can both save money and save the ecology."

The Role of Leader in Mobilizing Power

An authentic leader does not deny crisis; in fact, her actions may actually precipitate the crisis, make it more visible, more immediate. Martin Luther King, Jr. was accused of "starting trouble" when he led a group of marchers into a city. However, the violence was always there; he just made people own it (or disavow it). No more casual, anonymous late night lynchings. Do it on national television, do it with the world watching, do it in front of your minister, your children; do it unmasked.

The authentic leader keeps us from being overwhelmed by crisis. The authentic leader helps us to ride the waves of chaos which threaten to engulf us. The authentic leader does not tell us that life is easy; she tells us that life is difficult, that if we are not careful, if we are not willing to make sacrifices, that our choices, our inaction, may indeed engulf us.

> ***An authentic leader does not deny
> crisis; in fact, her actions may actually
> precipitate crisis.***

Some people only feel confident swimming in shallow water. As soon as they move into deeper water, they panic. The water is the same, whether five feet or five hundred. There is no difference in its ability to support; the only difference is in the perception of safety.

The authentic leader calls upon us to make sacrifices, to re-examine our comfort zone of perceived safety and move toward the deeper water.

Thou shalt love the Lord thy God with all thy heart, and with all thy soul, and with all thy mind. This is the first and great commandment. And the second is like unto it, Thou shalt love thy neighbor as thyself. On these two commandments hang all the law and the prophets.

—Jesus of Nazareth (According to Matthew)

Love, Compassion, and Leadership

Love and Compassion Are the Authentic Leader's Primary Motivation

The authentic leader operates from a basis of love and compassion. This is the essence of true leadership. If a leader is motivated by love, his actions will be correct, no matter what he does. If a leader is motivated by something, anything, other than love, his actions will be incorrect and inappropriate, no matter how well thought out, logical, or based on fact.

In order to fulfill our roles as spiritual leaders, we must operate from an inner well of love. We must love ourselves enough to take a good, long, realistic look at who and what we are, to operate from a basis of our strengths and to eliminate or transform our weaknesses. We must love others enough to see that, in the final analysis, there are no "others," just people who want the same things we want, but don't know how to get them.

43

Love conjures up cute, fuzzy bunny images. That is love—but so is the hurricane force which can cut us to the bone. For example, there was a story out of Boston of a woman who watched in horror as her five year old child stumbled and fell out of an open window in their four story apartment building. Acting at the speed of love, the mother raced to the window, reached out and grabbed the child in mid-air, and with one hand, hauled her back into the apartment. It was later discovered that the mother's grip was so strong she broke the bones in her daughter's arm. The force of that grip was love.

> **We must love others enough to see that, in the final analysis, there are no "others," just people who want the same things we want**

That is the kind of love that will transform the ghetto into a Third Millennium, livable community.

We can get caught up thinking that love is all hugging and kissing and positive relating. Sometimes that is love, but many other times it's just passivity, avoidance and denial. Because I love you, I will do certain things, take actions which may even produce short-term pain. Because the mother loves her daughter, she combs her hair, which for little black girls can be a sometimes painful experience. Doctors will break the legs of seriously bow-legged children, so that the bones can grow straight. One of my friends locked her drug-addicted brother in a closet for four days, forcing him to go "cold turkey." All of these are acts of love.

Love is my willingness to extend myself for another's growth. That definition, from M. Scott Peck's bestseller, *The*

Road Less Traveled, sums up the essence of love, and also distinguishes it from other emotional states. The man who wants to keep his wife dependent on him doesn't love her; the mother who does not want her child to grow up to an adult is operating from an emotional state other than love.

On the other hand, the man who supports his wife to go to school, or join a women's group, knowing full well that it may mean they spend less time together, is extending himself (his need/desire to be with her) for her growth (finding out who and what she is).

This type of love can appear to be negative, like the parents who "ground" their teenager when he or she is taking immature, needless risks with life and limb. To the teenager, this is harsh, cruel and unloving; to the parents, it is supporting her future growth with corrective actions now.

> **The willingness to extend for the growth of another can be, must be, the basis for domestic and foreign policy for our nation.**

The willingness to extend oneself for the growth of another can be, and it is the premise of this book that it *must* be, the basis for domestic and foreign policy for our nation. We see an example of this in the well-intentioned, although misguided attempts to end poverty in the sixties, or in the Cuban Missile Crisis, in which President Kennedy perceived a direct threat to this country and took swift, decisive action to correct it, essentially "grounding" the teenage Krushchev.

I know that I thoroughly confuse the Skinheads I run into, whether in Pioneer Square in Portland or Wenceslas Square in Czechoslovakia. I confuse them because I smile at them.

I smile, not from cowardice or defensiveness. Not a weak-willed, "please don't beat me up" smile. I make eye contact, human to human. I do that with everyone I meet; why would I treat them any differently? I look *through* their barriers of anger and militancy. And what happens is that they smile back. As a reflex, almost against their will, the human in them responds to the human in me.

Over a year ago, in my first encounter with Skinheads, my instinctive reaction was to freeze up, get defensive, raise my shoulders and lower my eyes in the "flight or fight" posture. Then I remembered: these are human beings. They have been hurt as children; they wear their pain on their sleeves. I can interact with them, be compassionate with them, at the level of their pain. I can look through their shields to the damaged child within. I do not condone their behavior but that does not mean they are no longer children of God. I do not condone the behavior of those walking down the street smoking cigarettes; I still smile and speak to them.

Can you imagine a world in which everyone acts out of love and compassion, instead of fear and pain?

Thich Nhat Hanh is a Vietnamese Buddhist monk who was nominated for the Nobel Peace Prize by Martin Luther King, Jr. In his book, *Being Peace*, this gentle soul tells of the horrors of the Vietnamese boat people, preyed upon by pirates in the South China Sea. He says that it is easy for us to be sympathetic to the victims; it takes a special kind of compassion to see the raping, thieving, murdering pirates as the little abused children who grew up into hard-hearted adults. It is that level of compassion, opening our hearts to all, which will set us on a path which leads to our true, mature humanity.

Opening ourselves to another's pain does not mean taking on their pain as ours. There is a space between being cold and aloof on the one hand, and being totally absorbed in the other. The first step in being compassionate is being balanced.

Can you imagine a world in which everyone acts out of love and compassion, instead of fear and pain? We hear our parents talk about the times when no one in the town locked their doors, when everyone left their keys in their car. Can you imagine a society which lays off policemen and has no standing army? That is our destination, once we stop reinforcing pain and start healing it.

The Pathways to Authentic Leadership

The Authentic Leader Serves the Universal Interest

Universal interest is the opposite of self-interest. The authentic leader recognizes that his interests are connected to the interests of everyone else on the planet.

The authentic leader does not avoid a threat to his own life in putting forth his principles. We see that occurring over and over again. Look at the times Martin Luther King, Jr., Rosa Parks, or Mahatma Gandhi put themselves directly in harm's way. They knew they could be physically injured or even killed by those who opposed them. That did not deter them.

At that point, personal self-interest dictates that you leave the situation, you avoid the pain. But the universal interest says that it is important that this act be done; it is important to stand against this injustice.

If it means that I am hurt, so be it. If it means that I am killed, so be it. At that point, the authentic leader has freed himself from those things society uses to control behavior.

That freedom is the basis of empowerment, which turns the leader into a force in the world.

The Authentic Leader Practices the Golden Rule

The leader practices treating others the way she wants to be treated. The leader practices "We Are One." My interests and your interests are so intertwined that I cannot help you without helping myself.

The continuing Congressional budget muddle is an example of practicing the law of expediency. The question perennially faced by the legislators is: how can you effect fundamental change without offending anyone? The answer? You can't.

Instead of practicing the law of expediency, the authentic leader creates "win-win" situations. Instead of doing what is expedient, the authentic leader does what is right.

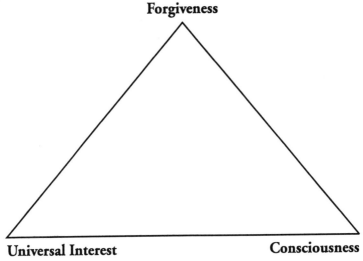

The Pathways to Authentic Leadership—The Outward Path

When I practiced law, my benchmark for a fair negotiation was whether the parties would be willing to walk around to the other side of the table and accept the settlement. If so, it was fair. If not, we continued work.

Instead of doing what is expedient, the authentic leader does what is right.

Our present society is based on "win-lose." People cannot even define how they win without defining how the other party loses.

Recently I had to run an errand to one of Portland's suburbs and found myself in a rush-hour traffic jam. At a major intersection, I faced a choice: I could pull out into the intersection, blocking traffic, or stay on my side of the light, allowing room for crossing traffic. Although the forty feet of asphalt in front of me was inviting, I stayed put. Traffic behind me welled up. I had to wait for two light changes before the traffic cleared.

The willingness to think about the welfare of others will get us through any crisis.

While sitting at the light, my thoughts went back to a similar situation in rush-hour traffic in Washington, D.C. On the East Coast, in the face of my choice to not block the intersection, scores of angry drivers started honking their horns, rolling down their car windows, and yelling obscenities at me. One driver about four cars back actually got out of his car and started walking menacingly toward me. (Fortunately, the traffic cleared right around then, enough for me to squeeze in without blocking traffic. Immediately, all of the drivers behind me surged forward, gridlocking the intersection.)

Sitting in the Oregon traffic jam, with its resignedly patient drivers, I realized that my fellow Oregonians were displaying the attitude which would get them through any crisis: the willingness to consider the welfare of others. The "me first" attitude of the east coast drivers escalates the most trivial situation into a crisis.

As I sat at that traffic light, I realized that each and every one of us will "face the light." What we do will reflect our values. No one knows what the future holds. The only way to prepare for the chaos is to develop inner balance, personal character and a healing outlook.

The Authentic Leader Is Forgiving

The authentic leader practices something the Tibetan Buddhist tradition of Shambala calls dra-la; above the enemy. Beyond the enemy. So far beyond the enemy that the authentic leader does not have an enemy. Like getting "beaten up" by a two year old, the authentic leader does not have an enemy because she cannot be hurt.

The authentic leader operates from the basis of "We Are One." If we are one, I can't have an enemy. If we all share the same problem, how can you be against me? As the organization Beyond War states, every conflict is a civil war, a war between brothers and sisters.

Look at the number of times Mahatma Gandhi stated that he wanted the British to leave as friends. He definitely wanted them to leave; make no mistake about that. But, he wanted them to be able to come back, to have fond memories of the friends they left behind.

If we are one, I can't have an enemy.

One of the things that marked the Czechoslovakian "Velvet Revolution" from the Romanian upheaval is that quality. When Vaclav Havel became president, one of his first acts was to make sure they did not create any enemies. Some Czechs wanted to conduct a witch hunt, find the old Communists, the secret police and the collaborators, put them on trial, punish them. Havel realized all were responsible. Havel said, "We cannot lay the blame on those who ruled us before, not only because this would not be true, but also because it could detract from the responsibility each of us now faces—the responsibility to act on our own initiative, freely, sensibly and quickly."

Compare the Czechoslovakian president's statement to what passes for leadership in the United States. Look around this country at the people who are so willing to lay blame. Look at the people who generate enemies in their lives. Look at the succession of presidents, from both parties, trying vainly to avoid responsibility and laying blame for their inept and inadequate domestic and foreign policies on someone else.

Unforgiveness means being locked in mortal combat with phantoms.

We accept skinheads, industrial polluters, driftnet fishers and social bigots as "the enemy." While I do not condone their behavior, I will not separate from them, I will not make an enemy of them. I will always treat them like the children of God that they are. And, like Gandhi and King, I will transform that person who thinks they are my enemy into my friend. There is an old saying that it's the biggest former sinners who sing loudest in the choir. Remember that it was the anti-Jesus, Roman apologist Saul who became Paul, the evangelist. Think about the powerful allies that the polluters, the racists, the ecological rapists will make when they are transformed into friends!

Is this so far-fetched? Look at the former segregationists who are now staunch defenders of minority rights. Look at the former male chauvinists who act as mentors for female executives. Once people see the light, they willingly make amends for past misdeeds.

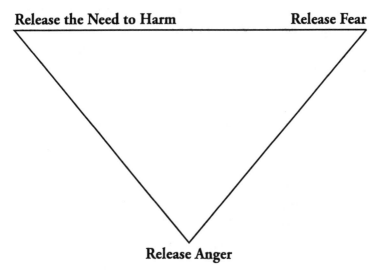

Release the Need to Harm   **Release Fear**

Release Anger

The Pathways to Authentic Leadership—The Inward Path

The Authentic Leader Has Released Anger

Anger is a force, not a power. In fact, anger is an expression of powerlessness. When you are angry, you are saying, "I do not have power." It is impossible to experience both power and anger. Outrage, yes. Anger, no.

Ten years ago, I directed a community development project in North Carolina; our goal was to buy out two major landlords. We needed over two million dollars to accomplish the purchase of over three hundred homes. We held our meetings in a beautiful African-American church, crowded with over three hundred residents. When I got to the part about money, everyone in the meeting choked. "The white man won't give us two million dollars!" Progress stopped right there. The residents saw the money as an insurmountable barrier. Total impasse.

We then went through a process of releasing limited thinking around their self-concept. They had made the ubiquitous "white man" the enemy, then imputed to that enemy intentions based on their own lack of self-worth. After several sessions of confidence building, they were able to walk past their fear, their lack of confidence, their anger, their powerlessness. They were able to achieve their goal; the "white man" provided all the capital they needed to accomplish that goal. They were able to release centuries of held-in repression.

Anger is an expression of powerlessness. People fear they will lose their identity if they give up their anger and hate. They need to create an enemy so they know they exist.

Some members of some groups (for example, blacks, Jews, women) so closely identify with oppression that subconsciously they feel they will lose their identity, their culture, if they release their hate, anger and frustration. Many blacks tell me that being black *means* being angry; that anger *defines* blackness.

The answer is to become peaceful, to release old, dysfunctional identities to allow a new, positive identity to emerge. Many techniques exist to release dysfunction, some of them centuries old. The particular releasing technique is less important than the willingness to engage the technique.

Releasing Anger: Moving from Protest to Power

Look at the number of folks who are involved in the "anti" movement. Anti-polluters, anti-racism, anti-drug dealers, anti-this, anti-that.

The question is: what are you for? What do you stand for? What are you going to do about this? Stop focusing on the rats: what does your cat look like?

**What we focus on gets stronger.
Focusing on the problem makes the
problem stronger.**

They reply: "If I don't focus on stopping the negative (apartheid, environmental pollution, etc.), it will get stronger." In fact, the exact opposite is true. What we focus on gets stronger. Focusing on the problem makes the problem stronger. In Vietnam, the United States focused on stopping the communists. The communists became stronger. Domestically, we have had the War on Poverty and the War on Drugs. Both poverty and drugs are more prevalent. In South Africa, although the form of violence is shifting from officially sanctioned brutality to unofficial acts of violence, the death rate is increasing because of racial and ethnic hate.

The authentic leader knows that protest is ultimately a recognition that power lies outside of the protester. It is a negation of the concept of interconnectedness, each of us is connected with the problem and the solution. Since it is a negation and rejection of power, it places power in the very hands of those who are being protested. Protest is a recognition of powerlessness.

Each and every person on this planet is a source of power. "There's nothing I can do about it!" is both a lie and a denial of our power and responsibility.

It is not death or pain or loss that robs us of power: it is the fear of death, the fear of pain, the fear of loss that turns the manipulated into victims and the manipulators into terrorists.

The Authentic Leader Has Released Fear

Fearlessness does not mean that you do not experience fear; it just means that you don't let it stop you from doing what you have to do. A fearless person recognizes and moves through her fear. She sees it, acknowledges it, then continues to walk past it. She then turns around and acknowledges that the fear was illusory.

A person who does not experience any fear is reckless, dangerous and probably in denial (or, a saint, of which there are few). The authentic leader still experiences the twinge of fear when walking the path of authentic power; she is just not stopped by it.

The authentic leader is fearless because she is dealing with her "stuff." She has clarified her values, her principles. She believes in what she struggles for. She places her principles as a priority in her life. She lives her principles.

> ### *Fearlessness does not mean that you do not experience fear; it just means that you don't let it stop you from doing what you have to do.*

There aren't any "hooks" for anyone to jerk the authentic leader around. The authentic leader is running on an internal gyroscope; she cannot be provoked or threatened or co-opted. The authentic leader is internally rich; there is no fear of loss.

> ### *Fear strikes at what you most value.*

Fear strikes at what you most value. Do you fear losing your life? You can be controlled by a threat to your life. Do you fear loss of material possessions? You can be controlled by a threat to those possessions. How about your fear of losing your social status, being seen as wrong, or bad, or foolish? You have another "hook" by which you can be controlled.

The hook remover is your ability to say "so what?" As Gandhi said, you wish to take my life? Then take it. (Hook removed.) As King said, you wish to ruin my family and social standing? So what? (Hook removed.)

When you cannot be controlled by others, you are experiencing the ultimate power. When people come together on the basis of being totally powerful, totally fearless, they become unstoppable. Gandhi called that collective energy the "soul force," or satyagraha. When people come together in the context of a positive, fearless mass experience, suddenly the world changes.

When you say, as Gandhi said, "If you kill me, you have my dead body, not my obedience," you are free. And, until you can honestly say this, you are not. As long as you think an lose something, you can be controlled. The Native Americans have a saying, "What a wonderful day to die!" A statement like that puts everything else into perspective.

Remember Karl Marx's statement: "Workers of the world unite; you have nothing to lose but your chains!" At the time he said that, back when "the workers of the world" didn't have Winnebagos, time share condominiums, and kids in college, that was a radical, powerful, liberating statement. Now, those workers are the pillars of the status quo, afraid to rock the boat, afraid of losing what they've got.

When you cannot be controlled by others, you are experiencing ultimate power.

The authentic leader is willing to personally suffer and experience setbacks for principles. King, Gandhi, and Havel were punished for their beliefs and outspokenness. Gandhi and King were threatened, jailed and ultimately assassinated. Havel was forbidden to write, forced to perform degrading work in a brewery, and imprisoned.

All three, and countless others, found the strength to maintain their principles while experiencing setbacks and pains.

The authentic leader is willing to address the tough issues. We know what has to be done in this country. We have to stop our over-consumption. We have to make our lives more fulfilling. We have to create a sustainable economy. We have to clean up the mess we have created, in our hearts, in our families, in our neighborhoods.

We know what to do. We know how to do it. The only thing we lack is the will to walk past the fear of the unknown.

Living within the Truth

Living within a Lie

In his book *Living in Truth*, Vaclav Havel talks about our declining civilization. The society we live in is essentially a lie. We all know that it's a lie. We continue to acquiesce in it. We act as though voting for a particular personality in Congress or going to the "right" protest rally is going to change the chaos we face. We know nothing will change, but we participate in the fraud. We act like buying a new car or the latest electronic gadget will make our lives better. We know this is a lie. We act like smoking the right cigarette, using the right mouthwash, or recycling our newspapers will cause us to feel fulfilled. Deep inside, we know nothing will change. But we participate in the fraud.

> **Authentic leadership comes from the moral force of character, not control.**

The person who is living within the truth doesn't care if others follow him. He marches to the beat of the different drummer. He does what he knows in his heart is right. He practices and models his values at all times. He acts fearlessly in the world. He has no enemies.

Authentic leadership comes from the moral force of character, not control. It was Havel's force of moral character that led and sustained the "Velvet Revolution." It was simply the force of his character that led to the downfall of the Czechoslovakian Communist regime. What did he do? What power did he have, rolling beer barrels in a Prague brewery, or writing a four page letter once a week to his wife while in prison?

It was the moral force of King's character that brought down US apartheid. What did he do? What armies did he have, besides armies of bright-eyed Sunday school children or college students? What power did he have, roughed up and thrown into jail, writing a letter on scraps of paper from his cell in Birmingham, a letter which spelled the end of American apartheid?

It was the moral force of Gandhi's character that brought down the British Raj in India. What power did a skinny little brown man in loincloth and sandals have? Who did he control? How could his simple decision to fast stop murderous mobs of Hindus and Muslims from hacking each other to death? How could his personal opposition bring down the most powerful military force in the world?

Authentic Leadership Comes from the Moral Force of Character, Not Control

Authentic leaders are able to exercise the moral force of character in the world, whether in the check-out line in the grocery or sitting in an office or leading the masses in a demonstration. They are always interacting with people at the level of the deep knowledge of their moral energy.

Being true to themselves, they are practicing and living their authenticity.

Healing the pain of dysfunctional living is a subversive act.

When the authentic leader speaks, her words are more than just the ideas running around in her head. Compare this to any recent US president, who hires the most skillful speechwriters to make it sound as though he were speaking from the field of universal consciousness. When Gandhi spoke, he could speak softly, plainly, from the heart. People heard him at deep levels of consciousness. People "got it." Vaclav Havel is a most unassuming revolutionary, cerebral, bookish, intellectual; this man led millions in demonstrations that overturned the status quo. His voice, although very mild and quiet, moves people to act. And, although Dr. King will go down in history as one of humankind's greatest orators, he didn't start out that way. Green, shy and hesitant, he grew into his role over time.

The authentic leader is willing to take and share responsibility. The authentic leader doesn't blame others for his own experiences. Instead of finding someone to blame, he looks for opportunities to share responsibility, share successes, and commiserate over setbacks. If his children are getting bad grades in school, he does not automatically blame the school system. He asks the question: what can all of us do, together, that will solve this situation? How can we all win?

Each of us is a spiritual being. Each of us has a spiritual practice (whether conscious or unconscious). Each of us has a moral force. Each of us can apply that moral force to solve the mega-crises of today.

The Authentic Leader Is Subversive

In a classic sense, my attempts at living an authentic life are subversive. Not in the sense of trying to bring down "The System" (I am learning to become indifferent to it), but in the sense that my decision to live an authentic life destabilizes and unsupports the "living within a lie" order, while supporting and nurturing "living within the truth."

The etymology of the word *subvert* is from Latin and French: *sub* meaning "up from under," *vertere* meaning "to turn." A subversive act is one that turns the status quo. From the bottom up. In these days and times, healing the pain of dysfunctional living is a subversive act.

Riding my bicycle is a subversive act.

Our actions either support the existing order, are neutral to it, or destabilize it. When I buy General Electric light bulbs, I am helping GE make weapons systems: once the money goes to GE, it props up their entire system. When I purchase a sandwich from Essential Foods, I am helping organizations like Intentional Futures and the Seattle Ecology House. Therefore, my consciousness of the power of every dollar I spend subverts the system.

I ride my bicycle, as an eco-political statement, as exercise, as primary transportation. There is a whole system of gas stations, traffic jams, parking lots, tire salesmen, road crews... an entire system that I unplug by climbing on my bike. If everyone traveling within five miles of home followed my example by either bicycling or taking public transportation, the auto-dependent system would collapse. Therefore, my riding a bicycle is a subversive act.

For example: I want to watch a video tonight. I could rent one from Video Mania, where I personally know the owner and many of the employees; where my money stays in the local economy, at least briefly. Or I can rent from Blockbuster Video, where despite their aura of corporate cheerfulness, my dollars go to support a corporate culture and a multinational mega-business. It's the same video.

Another example: I can buy my dinner veggie burrito from the tacqueria down the street, a small taco shop and Mexican market, where my dollars support the emergent Mexican community in my neighborhood. Although the owners and workers don't speak much English (and my Spanish is still meager), I have a sense of community and feeling at home.

Or I can buy a burrito from Taco Bell. The Taco Bell burrito may be cheaper, and have the remarkable sameness of industrial standardization. But which lifestyle do I support? Which culture do I support?

Part Five

The Rising Tide

A Sustainable Future in 20 Years—or 20 Months

There has to be a transition from late industrial society toward shared values, goals and understandings that fit in with rather than contend against the regenerative process of the biosphere. We need *to begin building a dwelling in life instead of on top of it.*

—Peter Berg (Speech at Portland Audubon Society, 1991)

4,000 Days and Counting

The year 2000 is almost tomorrow. Not some vague future, but now. The Third Millennium will happen *days* from now.

The decline actually sows the seeds for a new civilizational order.

The world is changing so rapidly, people are finding it difficult adapting to the new world. Anthropologist Mary Catherine Bateson said that virtually all of us are immigrants, born into a culture which no longer exists, finding ourselves strangers in a strange land. Especially for people who are trying to hold on to the old ways, the turbulent times can create dislocation and pain.

A New World Order

The new world order will not be found in the *New York Times* or on CBS News. By the time the "mainstream" media realizes the change, the change will be complete. And we all will be over the edge.

Signs of the new world order can be found in the transformative changes occurring within the former Soviet bloc countries and within the former Soviet Union. Examples can be found in the "Velvet Revolution" sweeping Czechoslovakia, which is ending its arms industry, putting 250,000 people out of work, because supplying arms to the Third World is an immoral act.

In this country, one of the signs of the coming new world order is the breakdown of large institutions, including banking, business and government. Once-mighty brokerage houses are failing; accounting firms are facing bankruptcy; banks are on the auction block; even the former pillars of commerce like Sears have fallen on hard times.

Many people treat these signs with alarm. However, Barbara Marx Hubbard talks about being able to recognize what is breaking through from what is breaking down. In his book, *Voluntary Simplicity*, Duane Elgin has a graph that shows the stages of civilizational decline. As one civilization falls, there is a rising curve for the new order. The decline actually sows the seeds for a new civilizational order. Our question is: which slope will we devote our attention to—the one declining or the one advancing?

The old society will turn into the humus for a new civilization.

Recently, a friend was commenting that he felt depression and despair from reading a certain article in the newspaper. I told him that I read the same paper and laughed. I am seeing that indeed the old society is continuing its collapse, making space for the new to emerge. I can feel hopeful about what is breaking through, by looking at what is breaking down.

The leaders of the new society must prepare for an abrupt shift in economic, social and political patterns.

In Earth's pre-history, when a dinosaur died, it keeled over, tail thrashing. Even in its death throes, it still packed the power to kill. The same is true for the old society; although it is dying, it still has the power to wage war, consume resources, tax us to death, etc.

For those who want to lock into the old society, who want to revive the dinosaur, it appears that the world is coming to an end. Jump out the windows, slit your wrists, drink the poison Kool-Aid: there is nothing left to live for.

As for me, I say let the old society die. It will turn into the humus for a new civilization. We are the leaders of the new civilization. None of us can predict the future with any accuracy; we don't know what it will look like, but we can be confident it will be more compassionate, more humane, more integrated, more fulfilling than the one we have. We will take the best of the old and merge it with the best experiments in living we are building now.

We, the leaders of the new society, must prepare for an abrupt shift in economic, social and political patterns. The changes could take as long as twenty years to fully manifest. On the other hand, the old society could unravel very swiftly, almost overnight.

There are several quick change scenarios which could bring the old society to a grinding halt. Most of the scenarios involve shortages of oil, money, or both. One way or another, it could all be over in three weeks.

The principal thing that Saddam Hussein did in invading Kuwait was to fast forward our crisis. He pointed out our addictions to us. He took the downward curve and shortened it, accelerating the decline. He made our dependencies and addictions visible. For that, we should thank him. He gave us our wake-up call. He gave us time to prepare.

I am sure that we will be living in a sustainable, ecologically and socially sane future within twenty years. Years ago, standing at what was left of the Berlin Wall, I was amazed at how rapid institutions can change. It can happen that fast here in North America.

We stand on the brink of the next evolutionary step for humankind.

A friend said to me that the decline in our society could go on another hundred years. I reminded him that this was the same prediction that Eric Honecker, the leader of the former East Germany, made a week before the wall came down. I asked my friend, "Are you prepared to become the governor of what is left of Oregon within five years? If you are not prepared, you better start thinking about it."

One of the world trends is the breakdown of the nation-states. Who is going to be the governor of Cascadia? That person will have just a little more lead time than the president of Lithuania, or the president of the Czech Republic or the president of Slovakia.

Toward Homo Sapiens Holonus

We are changing the way we see ourselves on the planet. That change will save us and our planet.

Homo erectus was a change from the humanoids who went before. The change was effected simply by standing up. The act of standing up changed the perspective of homo erectus; all of a sudden, they saw things differently. Their range of motion changed, improved. New outlooks developed. They were more appropriate to their environment.

We can imagine the reaction of the predecessors to the first emerging homo erectus: "Look at those fools standing up! They're unstable; they're gonna fall on their faces! Why waste all that energy! We've got a good system going; why rock the boat?"

My acts of self-preservation serve the entire planet.

The ones crawling around on all fours were no longer viable in the face of homo erectus.

Then came homo sapiens. They were able to look at a rock and see more than just a rock; they were able to see a tool in that rock, a weapon, a lever. This time, it is homo erectus who was clinging to the old ways, who was no longer viable for the times and conditions.

We stand on the brink of the next evolutionary step for humankind. Homo sapiens is no longer viable on this planet. We are seeing the emergence of homo sapiens holonus; the thinking humans who see themselves as part of the whole.

Holonus comes from a word introduced by Arthur Koestler: holon. A *holon* is a thing which is whole unto itself, which makes up greater wholes, and which itself is formed by smaller wholes. For example, I am whole, I have an identity unto myself; I make up greater wholes, other bodies (family, city, bioregion), and I am made up of smaller wholes (heart, lungs, blood). Each is a holon. I am conscious of being part of the whole. Descartes said, "I think, therefore I am." We now see his statement as the limited, inappropriate concept that it is.

My ability, as a good holon, to see myself as part of the whole, to see myself as part of you, makes me that much stronger, makes me (and other conscious holons) the more viable species. My acts of self-preservation serve the entire planet. I will do nothing to damage the holons which comprise "me." I will do nothing to damage the holons of which "me" is a part.

This is the philosophy of the "deep ecology" movement. To see ourselves as a part of ever larger (and ever smaller) wholes, to experience the connections between rain, tree and fish, to create a society based on harmony instead of greed, to perceive oneness—this is the destiny of homo sapiens holonus.

Practicing the Power of One—Right Now

So, after all is said and done, what is the Power of One? Specifically, what can you do, right now, to hasten the beginning of the new, Authentic Society? How do we begin to unhinge from the old paradigm? How can we begin the process which examines our relationships to both the problems and the solutions?

I've had a few years to ponder this question. As I have traveled around the country and into Europe and Africa, I have watched people's eyes light up when they hear or read the paradigm-shifting thoughts contained in this and other books. They have the same question: "What can I do!?! I'm ready to act now; what's the first step?"

My initial responses were less than satisfactory: "Look within." "Examine your own connections with the apparently dominant paradigm." "Open a dialog with your heart." All this seemed pretty weak-kneed compared to the magnitude of the problem.

When I arrived in Prague, Czechoslovakia, a few months after the Velvet Revolution, I remember standing in the center of Wenceslas Square, looking around and feeling deeply burdened by the enormity of changing a social, political, economic, cultural, even spiritual system that had been entrenched for over a half century. Where do you begin changing a system where nothing works? The task of transforming one relatively small Central European country pales to insignificance next to the challenge of changing the direction of the United States, the driving force of the global industrial paradigm.

But, as Lao Tzu said, the journey of a thousand miles begins with one step. We can shrink from the enormity of the task, never taking a step, or we can venture out, knowing that although we may not finish the journey, our children will.

The purpose of the following comments and suggestions is to take those first steps, to move us a little further on the road to authenticity. These suggestions will help us see our commitments on a practical level. (These "first steps" are part of an upcoming book entitled *Pioneering a New Society*. What follows is a brief exploration into concepts that will be more fully developed in that book.)

Ways to Support the Emerging, Authentic Society

As stated in previous chapters, authenticity is actually practicing one's values; an authentic person is willing to be held to the same standards by which they hold others. An authentic society consists of authentic people functioning together as a community.

You may already be doing many of the things suggested in this section. However, this section asks you to do those things with the consciousness that you are creating a new society by your action.

Changing Your Relationship to Time

Thomas Merton said that overwork is the most insidious form of violence that the nonviolent activist practices.

There is a pervasive form of contemporary violence to which the idealist fighting for peace by non-violent methods most easily succumbs: activism and over-work. The rush and pressure of modern life are a form, perhaps the most common form, of its innate violence. To allow oneself to be carried away by a multitude of conflicting concerns, to surrender to too many demands, to commit to too many projects, to want to help everyone in everything is to succumb to violence. The frenzy of the activist neutralizes work for peace. It destroys the fruitfulness of work, because it kills the root of inner wisdom which makes work fruitful.

—Thomas Merton

When I consciously slow down my life, I realize that time is as elastic or as brittle as I make it. I reduce my stress levels; I stop overworking; I allow time for wisdom to occur. Wisdom happens in a completely different relationship to time than the one demanded by the old paradigm. So you want to change the world? Become authentic in your relationship to time.

(An aside: I always find it interesting watching people who believe they are committed to fostering a new paradigm encounter native and indigenous people. When in meetings with Native Americans, I hear Anglos say: "Why don't they talk faster?" "Why doesn't he get to the point?" That is exactly the point!)

Another thing happens when you consciously alter your relationship to time: everyone around you notices. Those who feel that they are trapped by time will find in your example the courage to examine their own lives. When you become conscious of your relationship with time, you are claiming your power in a very dramatic way.

It is important in becoming conscious of time not to do this in a quirky or weird way. After all, people are indeed looking at you. If you want people to transform, you must create a model upon which people can actually pattern their lives. And the model must in some way be more attractive than what they've left.

If you slowed your life down, what do you believe would happen? Do you have mental tapes running that say you will in some way fail if you don't achieve certain things within a certain time frame? Who created that time frame? What would happen if you changed it? What would happen if the tapes were simply not true, that nothing bad would happen if you altered your relationship with time?

Even the term "slowing down" is relativistic; it implies that the current rate of old paradigm thinking and acting is "normal," and the way of living of our mothers and fathers for the past three million years is "slow." The alternative way of looking at this is that native and indigenous peoples' use of time is "normal," and we of the declining paradigm are hyper-accelerated.

Changing Your Relationship to Money

You economically support the old paradigm. So do I. It's pretty hard not to; the pervasiveness of the old paradigm means that the natural abundance and resources of our planet go to old paradigm maintenance and support.

Even the question, "What is money?" brings up some deep issues. Do you believe that "money" is something that is dirty, evil, better left alone? Do you believe money is your birthright, something that is a burden you must bear? Do you believe that money is something you work hard for, that you "earn?" Do you believe that people with money are inherently bad? Inherently good? Inherently powerful?

—Spend your money with human beings, not corporations.

—Pool your money in your community. Bank with a credit union or other local entity.

—Stop lending your money to multi-national corporations. You lend your money every time you put it in the bank. Lend your money to your friends. They will give you a higher interest rate than a bank's savings account, but much lower than the interest rate they are charged by a bank for a loan.

—Read Vicki Robin's book, *Your Money or Your Life*. This is a truly paradigm-shifting, consciousness-raising book on how to cure our addictive relationship with money.

Changing Your Relationship to People

Stop saying that "humans" are destroying the world. Humans have known how to live within the Earth's environmental tolerances for about three million years. The majority of humans on the planet *right now* know how to live within Earth's tolerances. It is the declining industrial paradigm that is destroying the planet.

Practice diversity. Really. I don't mean the easy kinds of diversity, like ethnic, sexual preference, or the like. The real test of diversity is ideological diversity: can you be tolerant of those who *think* differently than you? Not tolerant in order to change them, but tolerant in the face of those differences.

Practice authenticity with people. Don't let the electronic media buffer you. Face to face human contact, not through television, e-mail, Internet, or even telephone. These devices are useful, even necessary, but cannot substitute for human interaction.

Changing Your Relationship to the Law

This is an important point: those operating on a different cultural wavelength are seen as "outsiders" or "outlaws" to those who uphold the old paradigm. Skateboarders are criminals because they are outside the norm, not because they endanger.

We are creating new laws, new norms. Those norms will come up against the old paradigm; there will be a time of friction, and then a new set of laws will emerge.

Remember, Gandhi, King, Havel and other authentic leaders were criminals. Their commitment to follow a higher paradigm made them outlaws.

As I say to my teenage students, never get arrested for anything you are not proud of.

Changing Your Relationship to the Future

Visualize a community that works for all. (Stop visualizing the problem; you only make it stronger!) When creating your visualization, what is the place for people who are ideologically different from you? What is the place for your political, social, or ideological adversary? And, if you haven't created such a vision, do you truly believe in the strength that diversity offers?

Strengthen your visualization. Hold the vision every day. Create a ritual which grounds the vision and grounds you in the vision. See that there is something that happens every day that furthers the cause of your vision. Celebrate it!

Ground yourself in your present community. Join a community patrol or walking club. Learn the names, phone numbers and addresses of your immediate neighbors. Plan a neighborhood celebration. (Make sure you include the weird guy down the street who talks to himself.)

Share the vision with children. While the leading edge of the shift to an authentic society is happening now, it will take generations to fully manifest and for us to correct the damage done to our planet by the excesses of the industrial era. (Thinking that we will complete this work in our lifetimes is a legacy of the old paradigm.) Teach children to know that the manifestation of the authentic society vision is the most important thing that they can do with their lives. (If you don't have children, or if they are already grown, teach someone else's children—there are plenty out there looking for direction.)

Conclusion

If we are to survive in the 21st Century, we must wage a new struggle, the struggle for the soul of our country. We won't find it on the Moon or Mars. We won't find it in cocaine, a martini, or a bottle of cheap wine. We won't find it by trying to wage the Civil Rights struggle all over again, or fighting a war on the sands of the Middle East, or identifying domestic enemies.

New times and new issues call for a new direction. Let us honor the tremendous gains of the past, take responsibility for the errors of the past, but look forward to the challenges that lie ahead.

A few brave souls may venture a protest: "There's nothing I can do about the Middle East, or pollution, or why the price of everything is so high! I'm just one person; what power does one person have to change the world?"

The answer is easy: the power of compassion. When military might has rusted, when temporal fame has vanished, when all worldly powers have come to an end, the true power of compassion can be felt. Great cities turn to dust, beauty fades, the strong become weak and feeble, but the compassionate truly will inherit the earth. Who will history remember, Oliver North or Mother Teresa? Bull Connor, who gave the orders unleashing attack dogs on little black girls in Sunday school dresses, will be remembered in history, precisely because he was the antithesis of the man of compassion, Martin Luther King, Jr.

What can the compassionate do to correct our modern-day problems? Everything. Compassion is the light which drives out the darkness. Compassion wipes away the fears, making space for solutions to come forth. It is fear which makes us want to retreat; it is compassion that encourages us to expand, to realize that there is no separation between us and our problems—or our solutions.

Fear, egotism and arrogance cause us to ignore the pain and suffering of others. Learning compassion, that ultimately *I am you*, will provide the energy for the profound societal shift necessary for our salvation.

Afterword:
The Power of All

Since the time I wrote the first edition of *The Power of One*, much has changed in the United States. And yet, nothing has changed. We continue our inexorable march toward the chaos which is the seed-bed for our new civilization. Our crisis deepens.

I have changed. I find myself continuing to explore my own internal paradoxes. For example: while I continue to believe that community is the only way we will survive the deepening chaos, mostly I live alone. While I still believe that bicycling and public transportation are among the actions which will subvert the old paradigm, my own increasingly active work schedule requires that I travel by car and plane. I fervently advocate getting "off the grid," but find myself still emmeshed in the industrial paradigm.

(I write this at 30,000 feet, sharing an air-conditioned tube with a few hundred other souls, flying in excess of 500 miles per hour, gulping fossil fuels at the amazing rate of 1/2 mile per ten gallons. I'm working on a laptop computer, using software that makes Bill Gates even richer. I lie in the belly of the beast. I cross more territory in four hours than my great-grandparents could imagine traveling in a lifetime. I do this because I believe that attending certain meetings on the

East Coast were worth the damage I was producing, both in the biosphere and in my own body.)

To the dismay of some (and the comfort of most), I readily admit my imperfections. So to reiterate the introduction to this book: how dare I talk about the imperfections of the old paradigm when I am so deeply connected to it? Why do I talk so glibly about internal conflict and paradox?

The Function of Paradox

Paradox serves an incredibly valuable function in my life right now. *Acknowledging and accepting the paradox in my life keeps me from going crazy.* Paradox is my recognition that we are in the middle of a profound shift in consciousness, culture, and lifestyle. *In the middle.* Our lives were clear in the grip of the old paradigm. Our lives *will be* clear in the full bloom of the new paradigm of authenticity. In the middle? Paradox.

The most important thing about looking at paradox is that we recognize that we are living in two different and conflicting systems at once. I don't pretend that the old system has disappeared just because I'm recycling or giving money to environmental causes. At the same time, I acknowledge the emergence of a new consciousness, a new culture.

An authentic society is both an attitude and a choice. The attitude reflected by these paradoxes is that I want to live in a deeper and more spiritually connected society, a society which works for all. The attitude shift is that I set my intention and hold the vision for the authentic society, even when I find myself still acting in the old paradigm. The attitude shift is contained in my commitment to live in the new paradigm however and whenever possible.

The authentic society is also a matter of your choice. The countless actions which take place every day in your life all reflect your current mind-set and the choices you have made this day.

Recognizing paradox means that I acknowledge things are changing. Acknowledging change is very healthy. Until the change takes full shape, we are caught between two sets of behaviors, driven by two different mind-sets. Our behaviors are not fully appropriate to either paradigm. We are getting out of our pajamas, but not yet dressed in our street clothes.

The purpose of recognizing paradox is not to feel guilty or to be trapped in a sense of personal angst. This is not about judging myself. Paradox helps me to see the direction of my progress.

The Compassion of the Whole

> To the ordinary being, others often require tolerance [compassion]. To the highly evolved being, there is no such thing as tolerance [compassion], because there is no such thing as other.
>
> When you perceive that an act done to another is done to yourself, you have understood a great truth.
>
> —Lao Tzu, *Hua Hu Ching*

In the first edition of this book, I devoted two pages to the concept of holons: that we are each simultaneously part of larger wholes and smaller wholes. My trip to Africa in 1993 helped me to see that holon thinking deserves more than two pages; it should be the subject of an entire book. Holon thinking is the thing that will move us beyond dualistic, "us vs. them" compassion. Embracing what I've come to know as "the compassion of the whole" is the key to our survival.

In 1993, under the auspices of the United Nations, I traveled to Uganda as facilitator of a week-long training in community participation skills. I found myself teaching community concepts to people who had been living in community for thousands of years. I learned far more than I taught.

In a nutshell, one of the important lessons I learned in Uganda was that people were not individuated the way we are in the West. *Ugandans are holo-beings.* When they say "I," they mean something totally different from what Western-oriented people mean. This difference is so profound that in many instances I believe we don't understand each other, perhaps *cannot* understand each other. They have something incredibly rich to offer the West, but our arrogance and myopia prevents us from seeing it.

While in Uganda, I heard many stories about mothers giving their children to others, including "strangers," for care and safekeeping. I also had experience with Ugandan mothers "abandoning" their children, having no idea where their children were, or with whom they were staying. My Western-oriented thinking initially interpreted this as "bad parenting."

To the Ugandan mother, there are no strangers, and "abandonment" is a word that carries no meaning. The concepts of "stranger" and "abandonment" are based on individuation and duality. The African mother never gives her child to "another," no more than moving an object from one hand to another changes possession of the object. The Ugandan child never leaves the body of the mother, even though the particular part of "her body" that holds the child may not be consciously known. (Do you know exactly which of your pockets contains your house keys, or your wallet? Does it matter? If you can't tell me exactly where your keys are, does that mean you don't have them? If you can't tell me exactly which finger moves the "e" key on your keyboard, does that mean you can't type?)

This concept of being in a holonic relationship with others may be the norm for human interactions. Most of our ancestors who lived in wisdom traditions had this relationship. There are hundreds, perhaps thousands of tragic stories in this country where Native American parents had their children removed by various state child welfare agencies, because they could not state specifically where their children were. ("We left them in the village; Cousin Standing Bear might be with them. We haven't seen them for awhile.") The individual-oriented State considers this "abandonment," and cannot understand why the *entire village*, including the parents, protests the state putting the children in a foster home.

These two parents, a whole world apart, share something profound. They are integral parts of a large "holon-being." The Native American and the Ugandan mother do not see themselves as "on top" of the relationship to the larger Being. *The clan is "I." Sharif is a lesser (but important) "I." Sharif's heart is "I." Therefore, "I" is single-bodied, many-bodied and disembodied. The clan has a life beyond the life of each member. If you cut off an arm or cut out a gall bladder, "Sharif" will continue.*

My experience of the Ugandan holo-beings was by no means limited to parenting. Another quick example: the Ugandans I met would constantly question me on a concept they found baffling, *homelessness*. "How could a person be homeless?" they would ask. "How did the person's entire village die and leave that one person alive?" It took me a month to even begin to understand their questions about homelessness.

The universal nature of my Ugandan holon experience can be found in sacred traditions around the world, including the Sacred Hoop Vision of Black Elk, the Net of Indra, the kabbalistic "as above, so below," and Ezekiel's Wheel.

The experience of seeing a society, a culture of people who have lived in a holistic community which transcends our Western understanding, hammered home to me the power of one, in this instance, the power of the larger one. We then can see that social transformation through compassion to "others" is in reality merely a higher expression of self-love. When we understand and begin to encompass this expanded notion of power, we can begin to see that the power of one is in reality the power of all.

About the Author

Sharif M. Abdullah is a successful author, speaker, educator, workshop facilitator and catalyst. A former practicing attorney, Sharif has worked with thousands of individuals and facilitated scores of transformation, empowerment and leadership sessions for various public and private organizations, including the City of Portland, US Forest Service, the United Nations, and Freightliner Corporation. In addition, he has directed numerous community vision and empowerment projects, two of which have received national awards for citizen empowerment and public/private cooperation. He has worked with reluctant and hostile participants, replacing anger, powerlessness, stress, despair and violence with vision, empowerment, and freedom from fear.

Sharif is an adjunct faculty member at Marylhurst College and a lecturer at the University of California at Berkeley.

In addition to writing, speaking, and conducting workshops nationwide, Sharif is currently director of the Three Valleys Project, helping Anglos and Latinos bridge linguistic and cultural challenges to create collaborative community in rural Northwest areas.

Sustainable Living
Ecological Design & Planning
Resistance & Community
Environment & Justice
Nonviolence
Conscientious Commerce
The Feminist Transformation
Progressive Leadership
Educational & Parenting Resources

NEW SOCIETY PUBLISHERS

BOOKS TO BUILD A NEW SOCIETY